THE BEATLES' LANDMARKS IN LIVERPOOL

DANIEL K. LONGMAN

WITH COLOUR PHOTOGRAPHY BY BOB EDWARDS
FOREWORD BY BILL HARRY

AMBERLEY

Thanks to:
Bob Edwards
Anna Jackson
Alan Murphy
Simon Flavin
Birkenhead Reference Library
Liverpool Record Office
Sefton Information Services

First published 2017

Amberley Publishing, The Hill, Stroud
Gloucestershire GL5 4EP

www.amberley-books.com

ISBN 978 1 4456 5233 7 (print)
ISBN 978 1 4456 5234 4 (ebook)

Origination by Amberley Publishing.
Printed in Great Britain.

CONTENTS

FOREWORD

In 1958 I'd heard about a talented student at the art college called Stuart Sutcliffe. I got to know Stu and his friend Rod Murray as I always seemed attracted to talented people. I next noticed John Lennon in the college canteen and we became close friends. I took him to Ye Cracke, our watering hole, where I introduced John to Stu and Rod. We regularly visited the University of Liverpool where we could get cheaper drinks at the student bar. It was there where we all went to see Royston Ellis, advertised as a 'Beat poet'. This was due to the strong cultural influence in the UK at that time of the American Beat movement.

Afterwards at the Cracke we decided that Liverpool, too, was a culturally talented city, although no one would ever guess when considering the media. So, the four of us decided to make Liverpool famous: John with his music, Stu and Rod with their painting and me with my writing. We called ourselves the Dissenters.

We would visit the local pubs and coffee bars and the four of us were regulars in the Jacaranda in Slater Street. This was where I met my wife, Virginia, and the two of us began planning a magazine. Initially I thought of a jazz magazine, but getting to know Rory Storm, Johnny Hutchinson, Adrian Barber, Casey Jones and others at the club, I realised there was a music scene no one really seemed aware of. I wrote to the *Daily Mail* saying that Liverpool was like New Orleans at the turn of the century, but with rock 'n' roll instead of jazz. No reply of course, so Virginia and I started our own newspaper.

We rented an office at No. 81a Renshaw Street for £5 a week. Virginia gave up her job to work full time at £2.50 a week and I took no wages because I'd won the Senior City Art Scholarship and lived on that. I'd work round the clock, through the early hours, and it was early one morning that I came up with the name. When I was planning the area we'd cover, I visualised a policeman's beat – the Wirral, New Brighton, Crosby, Formby, Southport, Widnes, St Helens. This was my beat, so I came up with the name 'Mersey Beat'.

Distribution of the magazine began in earnest and on Thursday 6 July 1961, I walked into NEMS in Whitechapel and asked to see the manager. It was Brian Epstein. He ordered twelve copies and they sold out immediately, as did further orders. He took twelve dozen copies of Issue No. 2, of which the entire cover featured the Beatles recording in Hamburg, together with an Astrid Kirchherr image of them clad in black leather.

In his autobiography, Paul McCartney confirms this is when Brian first became aware of the Beatles. He asked to become my record reviewer and his columns began in Issue No. 3 while his adverts shared the same pages as Beatles features. Brian took me to lunch twice at the Basnett Bar in Basnett Street, all this happening months before the alleged claim that he never knew them until a boy came into his store asking for the record.

In November 1961, Brian asked me if I could arrange for him to visit the Cavern, which I'd told him was only around the corner from his shop. He didn't want to stand in a queue with youngsters and pay to get in, so I phoned Ray McFall and he arranged for Brian and his PA, Alistair Taylor, to enter. It was then that Brian saw the Beatles play for the very first time...

Bill Harry
Founder of *Mersey Beat*

Bill Harry seen presenting the Beatles with The Mersey Beat Poll Winner's Award on 15 December 1962.

INTRODUCTION

Like the waters of the Mersey, the Beatles have always been there (or at least that's how it feels). The Liver Birds, the football, the distinctive local accent, and the Beatles too have become ingrained into Liverpool's heritage and culture. Even today their omnipresent influence remains incredibly palpable with statues, pubs, festivals, museums, hotels and a whole lot more named or created in the boys' honour. My life began far too late to have ever witnessed the Beatles' amazing 1960s heyday myself, but as a history obsessive I felt compelled to delve into this unique and exciting period of Merseyside's past. *The Beatles' Landmarks in Liverpool* provides readers with the opportunity to see just some of the many places in and around the city associated with the band, alongside their twenty-first-century counterparts. Due to the prolific nature of the band's performances

After wowing Liverpool's club scene and taking the UK music charts by storm, the Beatles are seen here arriving to crack America in 1964.

and general galivanting, I have not been able to include every connected street, venue or related building. This is by no means a rebuff as to their individual importance or merit, but such places may perhaps feature in another publication in future. My aim when beginning this book was to show a succession of iconic locations dating from the Mersey Beat era so that readers may view such scenes as they would have appeared in the days of the Fab Four. A major frustration is that not every specific spot was deemed worthy of contemporary photography. In such instances, I have matched historic images as close to the original scene as possible. My thanks to Merseyside's local record offices, Mirrorpix, and the Salvation Army for their assistance in sourcing these views, and to Bob Edwards, who has captured their comparison in modern times. My appreciations also go to the army of authors past, whose knowledge and experience helped shape my own recent research. So, it is my privilege to be able to present to you *The Beatles' Landmarks in Liverpool*, in what is the 50th anniversary of the iconic Sgt. Pepper's Lonely Hearts Club Band, and the 60th anniversary of when Paul first met John. Their meeting changed the face of music forever, kick-starting a cultural renaissance in their hometown of Liverpool and indeed across the world. Their life, their music, and their legacy continues to captivate listeners of all ages and will no doubt be enjoyed for many more years to come.

Daniel K. Longman

1. LIVERPOOL WATERFRONT

Liverpool owes much of its success to its fortunate position on the banks of the River Mersey, which has been dominated by the Liver Building, the Cunard Building and the Port of Liverpool building since the early twentieth century. It is a thriving metropolis and one of Britain's most influential cities as a centre of culture, business and tourism, backed up by a rich heritage. The Liverpool of today is very different to the city's early beginnings, when the community was little more than a humble fishing village. The history of the city can be traced back to at least 1190 when the area was known as 'Liuerpul', defined as a muddy pool or creek. As the centuries passed the name evolved through various spellings, including Leuerepul, Lyuerpole, Lytherpole and Litherpoole. The pool refers to the inlet that once flowed across what is now the city centre and out into the Mersey.

Liverpool's trajectory into international importance began in 1207 when King John granted a royal charter giving the community borough status, along with associated rights and privileges. In time the waterfront allowed Liverpool to grow into what was the second city of the British Empire, playing a key role in the nation's slave trade and global business affairs. A steady growth in trade, combined with profitable connections right across globe, led Liverpool's population to boom throughout the Victorian era and the city rose to prominence. By 1900 Liverpool controlled much of the world's shipping with 40 per cent of all trade passing through here. This universal reach allowed Liverpool to embrace a variety of cultures, influencing the make-up of people and local customs, language and traditions. Liverpool is home to Europe's oldest Chinatown and was even one of the first British cities to experience the rhythm and blues sound of America's Deep South. As the century progressed, Liverpool's strategic importance led to the city becoming a target of the Nazi Luftwaffe, and it suffered catastrophic damage during the Blitz. Like many of the UK's northern economies, the city's reliance on industry led to a post-war crisis with the loss of many jobs and a significant reduction in the population. Locals looked for entertainment, and by 1962 over 350 bands were playing the pubs and clubs of Merseyside on a regular basis, creating what became known as Mersey Beat. The new sounds provided a platform for Liverpool to show off its talent and become a world leader in musical entertainment. A new boy band called the Beatles grew out of this new era of hedonistic optimism and the rest, of course, is history.

This stunning waterfront and the surrounding area is now designated as a UNESCO World Heritage site, and is a familiar vista to many. Today, the city is known for its great mix of attractions, and in 2008 it flourished as the official European Capital of Culture. Those celebrations were kicked off by none other than Ringo Starr, who performed from the roof of St George's Hall to 20,000 spectators. The former Beatle was joined by a cast of more than 1,000 performers to launch the year of culture, singing his new single, 'Liverpool 8' – a reference to the district where he grew up. The year featured hundreds of events and performances, with some of the more unusual sights being an assortment of bright-yellow superlambananas. Also on show was a giant mechanical spider named La Princess, which climbed down buildings, scurried through the streets and delighted the hordes of people who came to see it. The year 2008 also saw the opening of the Echo Arena, overlooking the river, as the city's premier entertainment venue. It was there that Liverpool played host to the MTV Europe Music Awards, featuring a number of artists, including Liverpool's own Sir Paul McCartney. He also played a gig at Anfield football ground as part of the Liverpool Sound Concert. The city's Capital of Culture status was a real catalyst for change and helped transform the reputation of Liverpool from a tired northern community in decline, to a world-class city on the rise. The city's musical heritage has undoubtedly helped bring about this shift, and even today the music of the Beatles and the sights and sounds of their Liverpool haunts draw in thousands of dedicated fans every year. A recent study revealed that the band's legacy generates over £80 million a year for the local economy, and supports over 2,000 jobs in the tourism and hospitality industries. After all these years, the Beatles are still very much a part of Liverpool life.

The city's famous waterfront with its iconic Three Graces overlooking the River Mersey.

Liverpool has grown to become one of the world's most renowned destinations of the twenty-first century.

2. MENLOVE AVENUE

The 1960s photograph opposite shows a typical stretch of Woolton's Menlove Avenue, the place where John Lennon called home. The road was named after Alderman Thomas Menlove, who had served on the local council and acted as chairman of the Health Committee around the turn of the twentieth century. No. 251 was built in 1933 by a local firm of builders, J. W. Jones, who were very prolific in this particular neighbourhood. The house was designed as a smart and uniform semi-detached property destined for the middle-class market – certainly not the common Scouse slums John would later become associated with. No. 251 was also known as Mendips after the limestones hills of Somerset, and no doubt a suitable moniker for such a well-to-do locality. John's aunt, Mimi Smith, kept the name after she moved in with her husband George as a sign of the family's seemingly upward mobility.

The house was to be John's home from the age of five, after doubts were raised about his mother Julia's ability to care for him. His room was the smallest, situated just above the front door to the house. Mimi was a keen reader and her passion for literature passed to John, who enjoyed reading works of every genre and even the local press. The Smiths made ends meet by renting out the spare room to young students, often males who Mimi deemed to be tidier houseguests. The couple had an arrangement with the University of Liverpool, who usually sent over students in pairs and used the dining room for meals and study. Their presence at Mendips no doubt influenced the young John, especially when one musically minded academic offered him use of a harmonica. It was here where John's early love of music began to become apparent and was later nourished by songs such as Elvis's 'Heartbreak Hotel'. Later, when the band began to practise round at John's house, Mimi had the porch enclosed to help block out the noise.

During his teenage years, John's relationship with his mother improved, but no amount of contact could make up for her absence in John's early upbringing. By the time John was seventeen, Julia had become a firm fixture back in his and Mimi's life. On the Tuesday evening of 15 July 1958, Julia had been visiting her sister at Mendips when the time came to say goodbye. At around 10 p.m., Julia left through the front gate and headed in the direction of the bus stop to catch the No. 4, which was due at any moment. Mimi hurried back outside in seconds after hearing a commotion, and was devastated to find her sister lying flat in the middle of Menlove Avenue – dead. She had been hit by a car. John was not at home at the time but on hearing the news he travelled to Sefton General Hospital; however he could not bring himself to look at his mother's body. Julia had been hit by a young off-duty police officer who should not have been behind the wheel without an accompanying qualified driver. He was, however, later acquitted of all charges, leaving John feeling resentful towards authority, as well as devastated at the loss of his mother once again.

A typical suburban stretch of Woolton's Menlove Avenue as seen in the 1960s.

John left Mendips after gaining a place at the Liverpool College of Art, moving out of his small bedroom and into student accommodation. He made a brief return home with his new bride Cynthia in the early 1960s, taking over what had been Aunt Mimi's dining room. Of course, this arrangement would not last forever. In 1965 – at the height of Beatlemania – John purchased a beautiful six-bedroom bungalow in Poole, Dorset. Harbour's Edge, as it was known, was to be Mimi's home until her death on 6 December 6 1991. It was her escape from the less enjoyable aspects of John's astronomic rise to fame and the crowds of autograph hunters who often lined the roads around Menlove Avenue. Back in Liverpool, she had once admonished her nephew's obsession with music with the words, 'The guitar's all very well John, but you'll never make a living out of it.' How wrong she was! John has those words printed and framed, and put on the wall as a cheeky housewarming present.

On 8 December 2000, to mark the 20th anniversary of John Lennon's death, English Heritage erected a blue plaque outside No. 251 to mark the importance of the house in cultural history. This was the first such plaque outside of London. Since his Aunt Mimi's departure, No. 251 Menlove Avenue has passed through a succession of owners; in 2002 the house was purchased by Yoko Ono, who donated it to the National Trust. The heritage champions set about a programme of refurbishment, which saw the property restored to

John Lennon's childhood home stands at No. 251 and is now owned by the National Trust.

the late 1950s style John would have known. The house is an unmissable stop on any Beatles tour and is open to visitors. Guests are shown around the house via the side door as it is said that Mimi would never have allowed visitors to enter via the front for fear of her carpets being ruined. Once inside, fans can see the very rooms where John lived out his childhood and adolescence, and where famous tracks such as 'Please Please Me' were first dreamt up all those years ago.

3. FORTHLIN ROAD

Forthlin Road lies in the green suburb of Allerton, a short drive south from the city centre. This was the setting for Paul McCartney's adolescent years and the home he grew up in with his brother Mike and father Jim. The house had originally been constructed in 1949, but it wasn't until the spring of 1956 that the McCartney family moved into No. 20. It was a relatively small council house, part of a terrace, but it provided for all the needs of the family. Paul's mother, Mary, worked as a midwife, and, as the house came with a telephone, it allowed her to be on call whenever she was needed. The couple had never been wealthy; Jim worked as a lowly salesman in the cotton trade and it wasn't until the Queen's coronation that they decided to invest in a television set. Tragically, Mary died of breast cancer just one year after moving in, leaving her husband to bring up the boys alone. There was help from aunties Milly and Gin but no one could truly replace the mother who had passed away aged only forty-seven.

Paul had been encouraged to learn the trumpet, but soon realised he would never be able to sing with a trumpet pressed to his lips. He asked his dad if he could swap it for a guitar. It was to be a basic, but adequate, Rex acoustic. Forthlin Road offered Paul the perfect place to practise his music and learn the craft that would ultimately gain him worldwide fame. Jim advised his son that he should also learn to play the piano and take up lessons; however, Paul preferred to learn by ear and could often be found listening to tunes on the family's Bakelite radio or learning from his friend Ian James. When Paul began to associate with John Lennon and his band, the Quarrymen, the teenagers used to secretly gather at Paul's house to practise when Jim was out at work. The bathroom provided surprisingly good acoustics and was the scene of much of Paul's early creativity. Many of the Beatles' best-known songs were composed at No. 20 Forthlin Road; for example, 'Love Me Do', 'I Saw Her Standing There' and 'When I'm Sixty-Four'.

The McCartney's time in Allerton ended in 1964. That year Paul returned from the band's tour of America and announced that he had brought a little house over on the Wirral. This was not for him, but a gift for his dad. The world had gone mad with Beatlemania and No. 20 Forthlin Road had become the focus of much of that attention. Fans could often be found camping outside the property, waiting to catch a glimpse of the famous family – perhaps even Paul himself. Jim had mentioned how he was starting to feel uncomfortable with people peering through the window and was becoming a victim of his son's extraordinary success. Late one night, under cover of darkness, the family possessions were packed into a removal van and sent off through the Mersey Tunnel to Rembrandt, a mock-Tudor detached house in Heswall, which would afford the family a greater degree of privacy. Jim would live there with his second wife, Angela, and his adopted daughter, Ruth, until his death twelve years later.

This house at No. 20 Forthlin Road was the home of the McCartney family from 1955 to 1965.

The property is also owned by the National Trust and is open to visitors for guided tours.

After the McCartneys moved out of Forthlin Road, the Joneses moved in. Sheila and Ashely Jones brought the house for £55,000, assuming that the visitors would stop now that the McCartneys had gone, but the couple found themselves becoming unofficial ambassadors for the family and the musical legacy they had left behind. In the 1970s, Mrs Jones decided it was time for a change and began to modernise the house by upgrading the property's windows and doors. These fittings are now highly sought-after collectors' items, with Paul's bedroom door once selling for nearly £3,000. The old front door, still a shade of its original green, sold for more than £5,000. After more than thirty years of residency the Joneses finally decided to move to a less-renowned property, and sold the house to the National Trust for a mere £47,000 in 1998. Due its importance in the story of international music, the National Trust broke away from its tradition of taking on historic country houses and recognised this small, unassuming council house in the suburbs of Liverpool to be something extra special. Today, visitors are welcomed into No. 20 Forthlin Road and can tour the property with the help of a live-in custodian. The interior has been restored to how the rooms would have looked during Paul's formative years and stands as a fascinating example in its own right of northern post-war housing.

4. UPTON GREEN

George Harrison was born on 25 February 1943 to Harry and Louise. He was the youngest of four children whose birth only added to the cramped living conditions the family already struggled to cope with.

In the 1950s, Upton Green was a newly built housing estate in the suburb of Speke offering somewhat standard council accommodation. To the young George Harrison, his new home at No. 25 was like a mansion. This was only the second house he had ever known, having moved from Wavertree's Arnold Grove at the start of 1958. His old terrace house was a tiny two-up two-down with a basic backyard. Now at Upton Green, the six-year-old was able to run around from room to room and the long rear garden; there was even the novelty of an indoor toilet. The Harrisons had been on the council's housing list for eighteen years and it seemed that their wait had finally paid off, yet the family were soon back to the authorities asking to be rehoused once again. Upton Grove was built around a large grassy oval centre where local kids would make a nuisance of themselves, even sometimes uprooting the plants Louise had planted in their front garden. George continued as a pupil at his original primary school of Dovedale, before moving up to the Liverpool Institute. His daily commute brought him into contact with fellow student Paul McCartney, who, after developing a good friendship, decided George should speak to John about joining the band. The pair met on the top of a double-decker bus, joined by Paul and the rest of the Quarrymen. George impressed the group with a rendition of the American classic 'Raunchy' and, despite some reservations about his age, George was asked to join as the band's lead guitarist. An added bonus to his membership was that Upton Green offered the boys a ready-made rehearsal space. George's mother was a big fan of their early type of music and recognised the band's potential almost immediately. On occasions she would even provide a little drop of whiskey for the boys to assist in their songwriting and rehearsals. On 20 December 1958, the band played here for the wedding reception of George's elder brother, stunning the older members of family with their new and unexpected style of entertainment.

The Harrisons did eventually move out of Upton Green, but it took another thirteen years for the family to be relocated to No. 174 Mackets Lane, Woolton. By this point George was a young nineteen-year-old with celebrity in his sights. He would soon be living in London enjoying the superstar lifestyle, but he frequently came back up north to spend time with his parents. It has been said that the Harrisons were the least private of all the families, and George's mother would personally respond to the mountains of fan mail that arrived at their door, even inviting people into her home for tea and biscuits and to chat about what it was like bringing up a Beatle.

A young George Harrison seen outside his home in Upton Green, guitar in hand.

George's childhood home in Speke was passed on to a succession of new tenants, each of whom modernised the property as time went by. In the autumn of 2014, the house had become freehold and was put up for sale by the owner. The event attracted worldwide attention when, on the evening of 20 October, the house was put up for auction at the Cavern Club. There had been a guide price of £100,000 but the successful bidder was a huge Beatles fan who, after once missing out on buying John Lennon's former home of No. 9 Newcastle Road, was happy to pay £156,000 for George's old abode. In 1965, George brought his parents their very own bungalow in the village of Appleton, near Warrington, where they remained for the rest of their days.

A similar view shows the neighbourhood of George's childhood in more modern times.

5. ADMIRAL GROVE

Richard Starkey (aka Ringo Starr) was born on 7 July 1940 in Madryn Street, but it was moving into No. 10 Admiral Grove that remains as one of his earliest memories. His mother Elsie rented the rather basic two-up two-down terrace after her husband left her to bring up the baby alone. They had left Ringo's birthplace, just a short distance away, after the breakdown of his parent's seven-year marriage. That, too, had been a very modest little property – located in the Dingle area of the city. Elsie's status as a single mother with a young child to support was not an enviable position, and she was forced to take on a number of odd jobs to put food on the table. This included a position as a barmaid at the nearby Empress pub.

Things were certainly not easy for the Starkeys, or for the rest of Liverpool, at this time. Richard would often be ushered into basements to avoid the threat of German bombers flying overhead, to be found later playing among the rubble once danger had passed. Disaster came later when he was struck down by a bout of appendicitis, which, due to complications, developed into peritonitis and a ten-week coma. The condition forced Richard to stay in hospital for just over a year and set his education back considerably. The lad had never been academically gifted, but after eventually returning to his classes at St Silas School the effect of his long absence was clear. Richard could barely read or write and was given extra help by a fellow classmate at home in the evenings. When he was fourteen his mother remarried, this time to London divorcee Harry Graves. Harry was a painter and decorator by trade and had secured a job at Burtonwood serving American aircraft. His income allowed Elsie to quit her myriad of jobs and spend more time at home. Harry was a tremendous influence on his stepson, who enjoyed reading comics he brought back from the base and listening to big band sound and American jazz.

In 1953, the very same year of his mother's marriage, Richard caught a cold that worsened into turberculosis. His health was once again at risk and he was sent to recover at the Royal Liverpool Children's Hospital on the Wirral. His stay lasted two years and is also where he is believed to have first taken an interest in drumming. On Richard's return to Admiral Grove he was given a big one-sided bass drum, but it was only good for playing during family gatherings with firewood as drumsticks. The future Ringo Starr would have to wait until Christmas 1957 before he was presented with a proper kit – with a snare drum, bass drum, hi-hat, tom-tom, cymbal and bass-drum pedal. Practising upstairs in the tiny terraced house quickly became frustrating for everyone. Richard's next step was to get some lessons and maybe even join a band.

No. 10 Admiral Grove still stands, but is no longer in possession of the family. Richard's twenty-first birthday would be the last he would celebrate at the house, when, on 7 July 1961, sixty invited guests miraculously squeezed into the property. Well-wishers included

How Admiral Grove appeared to Ringo Starr growing up in Liverpool 8.

musicians from the Hurricanes, Gerry and the Pacemakers and Richard's close friend Cilla White (later Cilla Black). Cilla herself was no stranger to the house and could be found at No. 10 Admiral Grove every Wednesday practising her hairdressing skills on Elsie Graves. Richard's talent for the drums provided a way out of the poverty he had been born into, not just for himself, but for his family. His early success with Rory Storm and the Hurricanes saw him settle on the stage name 'Ringo' due to an excessive love of jewellery and 'Starr' simply as a shortened version of his surname. His parents, Elise and Harry, stayed at the house until 1965, moving out to nearby Woolton. Ringo paid tribute to his Dingle roots in his 2008 album *Liverpool 8*, in which he references his birthplace and the need to escape to bigger and better things. In more recent times the house had been the home of Margaret Grose, who sadly died after nearly forty years of tenancy. She would happily welcome visitors into her home and show fans around for a small donation to the Linda McCartney Centre. The property has since been sold at a specialist auction held at the Cavern Club, where it sold for £70,000. His birthplace around the corner in Madryn Street also survives, but only just. The street sits within what has become collectively known as the Welsh Streets in memory of the Welsh immigrant community that originally settled here in the nineteenth century. In 2015, Liverpool City Council attempted to

Ringo's childhood home was sold in 2016 for £70,000 at an auction at the Cavern Club.

demolish 217 of these old Victorian terraces as part of a £15 million regeneration scheme, including the Starkey's house at No. 9. Calls for the council to reconsider were eventually heeded by the government, who stepped in and saved the buildings from the bulldozer. The official reason cited for the intervention was the potential effect on the appreciation of Liverpool's Beatles heritage, the site being the birthplace of Ringo Starr. The Welsh Streets are now awaiting an alternative conservation scheme to be implemented, which should better reflect the importance of this area and its contribution to the history of modern music.

6. THE LIVERPOOL INSTITUTE

The Liverpool Institute has been a feature of the Liverpool landscape for nearly 200 years. Over the decades its tutors have taught generations of local families and provided a good grounding for thousands of gifted adolescents. Based in Mount Street, construction began in 1825 as a Mechanics' Institute set up to provide educational opportunities to working-class men through evening classes. The building was designed by the architect A. H. Holme in a Greek revival style with a classical stone façade, intended to stimulate aspirations for knowledge and wisdom. The school grew to become a respected place of learning, with notable guest speakers such as the American essayist Ralph Waldo Emerson and the literary genius Charles Dickens.

By the mid-nineteenth century a boys' lower and upper school had been established, along with a library. From the more creative evening classes evolved an art school, and to reflect the additional teaching the institution changed its name to the Liverpool Institute and School of Arts. In 1905 the council took over the running of the school, which by that time had become the Liverpool Institute High School for Boys. It served as a traditional grammar school with many of its alumni going on to gain distinctions at Oxford and Cambridge as well as the University of Liverpool. However, the institute's most famous sons achieved their fame far away from academic pursuits. Paul McCartney took up his place in 1953, closely followed by George Harrison the following year. The boys met on the same bus to town from Speke and the two quickly became good friends. Paul recalled: 'George was a bus stop away. I would get on the bus for school and he would get on the stop after so, being so close to each other in age, we talked, although I tended to talk down to him because he was a year younger.'

Despite passing the required eleven-plus exam to gain a place at the institute, it is said that the teenage George was disinterested in his studies and often attempted to shed the prescribed uniform in favour of his own attire and trendy hairstyle. The young wannabe musician felt particularly disappointed at the lack of guitars in music class and showed little motivation for anything other than art. Paul, however, was by all accounts a more studious pupil, having achieved respectable passes at O level and later with A levels in English and Art. With the introduction of comprehensive education in the 1960s the school became devoid of purpose and fell into a spiral of decline. Its doors finally closed in 1985 after years of fruitless debate over its future and potential use. Standing empty, decay set it in and this once splendid building became an increasingly desolate eyesore. Fortunately, a nostalgic visit by Paul McCartney to reminisce over his formative years sowed new seeds of life for the old school. On viewing the building late one night while writing 'Liverpool Oratorio', the former student was horrified to see the deterioration it had suffered and vowed to bring this grand historic structure

Above: The Liverpool Institute on Mount Street captured on film in the 1960s.

Below: The building is now used as classrooms and performance space for the Liverpool Institute of Performing Arts.

back from the brink. A conversation with friend and producer George Martin led Paul to contact the entrepreneur Mark Featherstone-Witty, who was seeking help with a new educational venture. Mark had been inspired by the iconic New York dance film *Fame* and wished to create a similar performance school here in the UK. As luck would have it, Liverpool Council was seeking ways to build upon Liverpool's reputation as a city of music and boost this exciting aspect of Liverpool's heritage. Paul and George's old classrooms offered the perfect space. After many hours of planning and fundraising, as well as the renovation and partial rebuilding of the original structure, the Liverpool Institute of Performing Arts (LIPA) was complete. During the works the impressive frontage was returned to its former glory and many other historic features, such as the huge ionic columns, were cleaned and restored. The institute was formally opened by Her Majesty the Queen in the summer of 1996 following a multi-million-pound renovation scheme to transform the interior into a state-of-the-art performing arts establishment. LIPA was also the location from where Paul chose to give his acceptance when he was knighted, dedicating the award to the people of Liverpool and his bandmates. Each year masses of applications are received from aspiring students from around the world each hoping to gain a place to study here. Degree courses include Acting, Community Drama, Dance, Music Theatre and Entertainment Management, Music, Sound Technology, Theatre and Performance Design and Theatre and Performance Technology. Thanks to Paul and his team of dedicated collaborators, this wonderful Grade II-listed building has once again been put to good use, helping to educate future generations of artists and performers.

7. STANLEY STREET

Stanley Street was originally named after one of Liverpool's most influential families, whose links to the city date back to Elizabethan times. In the eras that followed, the thoroughfare became laden with industry and warehouses, as well as becoming home to the community's first synagogue in the mid-eighteenth century. This area suffered significant bombing during the Blitz, which resulted in the loss of Liverpool's head post office and other large-scale buildings. Stanley Street lies in the city centre and runs alongside Mathew Street. In the days of the Beatles, this was the location of Frank Hessy's music shop. Its close proximity to the Cavern Club allowed the wave of new Mersey Beat bands easy access to instruments and equipment, as well as upgrades and repairs.

The Hesselbergs opened their first shop in Manchester Street in the 1920s, but it was in their newer Stanley Street branch where Mimi came with John in 1957 to purchase his first real guitar. It was £17 – back then no small sum – but Hessy's was renowned for its generous credit agreements. Chief salesman Jim Gretty could also be very persuasive. He had earlier suggested to his boss that throwing in some free lessons would be good for business, so every week Jim would spend an hour teaching a group of thirty or so wannabe musicians how to play. Hessy's was also the place where Stuart Sutcliffe got his Hofner President guitar using money he raised from the sale of his work, *Summer Painting*. It caught the eye of wealthy businessman John Moores during an exhibition at the Walker Art Gallery in 1960. After moving into Gambier terrace with Stuart during their college days, Lennon convinced him to invest the cash in the guitar and join his band. They were sorely in need of a drummer and a bassist, so Stuart opted for the bass. By the time Brian Epstein took over as the Beatles' manager, the total credit bills had amounted to over £200. Brian kindly paid this all off out from his own pocket. Stuart's ability to play the bass improved over time, but his skill left a lot to be desired. 'It was a bit ropey, but it didn't matter at that time because he looked so cool,' George later remarked.

Hessy's music shop endured until in 1995 when it finally ceased trading after over sixty years in Stanley Street. At the present time the property is occupied by a jewellers, with the old entrance now part of the shop window display. Stanley Street retains much of its Victorian splendour but this too has been converted to accommodate new uses, with many of the buildings now home to offices and retail.

Beatles fans don't just come to this part of the city to see the remains of the former music shop; since 1982, a rather special life-sized statue of Eleanor Rigby waits to greet visitors from her stone bench. Eleanor's existence is all down to a musical contemporary of the boys, Tommy Steele. He was so keen to honour the work of the Beatles that he offered to create the sculpture for a token sum of 3d. This was a reference to his film musical *Half a Six Pence*, which had been released way back in 1967. Of course, the bronze

Above: Over the years the area's tall Victorian warehouses have given way to less industrial use.

Below: Hessey's music shop is no longer in business and its premises has since been converted.

A busy section of Stanley Street as it would have appeared in the days of the Fab Four.

A life-sized bronze statue of Eleanor Rigby welcomes visitors from across the world.

statue of Eleanor Rigby herself pays homage to the band's eponymous hit, which is seen by many as a lament for the lonely living in post-war Britain. A plaque inscribed upon a wall reveals that this statue is also dedicated to 'all the lonely people'. The Liverpool Beatles Appreciation Society once lobbied the City Council and Mayor Joe Anderson to move the sculpture to a more prominent location. They argued that her position on the fringes of the Cavern Quarter was too isolated and she should be relocated to make the best of her prestige and status in Beatles history. The request has so far been unheeded, and Eleanor continues to sit alone feeding the birds on her bench in Stanley Street.

8. ST PETER'S CHURCH, WOOLTON

It was Woolton's St Peter's Church that provided the backdrop to what is probably the most important meeting in the entire history of the Beatles. It was within these grounds on 6 July 1957 that Lennon and McCartney first met at a humble church fête. This was held in honour of the new Rose Queen and there was to be a display by the Liverpool police dogs, a fancy dress parade, side shows, and, of course, music. Fifteen-year-old Paul had been told that a local skiffle band calling themselves the Quarrymen would be playing and it might be a fun way to spend the afternoon. Paul cycled the ten minutes or so to the church and followed the distinctive sounds of 'Come Go with Me' by the Del Vikings, which he could hear coming from the field behind. In that field stood John Lennon, aged sixteen singing confidently into the mike. He was surrounded by his fellow Quarrymen: Eric Griffiths on guitar, Colin Hanton on the drums, Rod Davies on banjo, Pete Shotton on the washboard and Len Garry played a tea chest bass. Paul was impressed how the teenage vocalist was able to throw in his lyrics, but the truth was John hadn't memorised all of the words and was just making them up as he went along. Nevertheless, he had charisma and he was a natural showman. The Quarrymen were booked to play again that evening, just across the road at the church hall. Paul stayed to watch and was able to spend some time with John discussing his own musical abilities and teaching the band how best to tune their instruments. To the young Paul, John seemed so much older and experienced, with his unkempt hair and rock 'n' roll attitude. It was a moment that both boys would remember for the rest of their lives. By October, Paul was officially part of the band, making his debut at the New Clubmoor Hall, Norris Green.

St Peter's Church also housed another important connection to the history of the Beatles, whether they knew it or not. In the graveyard stands a headstone to a woman by the name of Eleanor Rigby. She passed away in 1939 and was buried in a family grave with several of her relatives. Paul has always maintained that the idea for his 1966 hit 'Eleanor Rigby' came out of the blue, but accepts that he may well have been subconsciously influenced from his days hanging about the cemetery years before. In 2008, a historic document believed to bear the signature of Miss Rigby was auctioned for charity. It was found in a Corporation of Liverpool accounts book and shows payment received by sixteen-year-old scullery maid E. Rigby to Liverpool's City Hospital. Her headstone has become a beacon for Beatles fans from across the world, with thousands travelling to this otherwise sleepy suburb to take a look.

St Peter's remains in regular use and provides a place of worship for the people of Woolton and further afield. Before 1826 the nearest church was nestled away in Childwall, some 6 miles away. It was decided a chapel was needed in Wooton, so it was in that year that the foundation stone was laid near to where the present-day church can now be found.

Above: The grounds of St Peter's Church provided the setting for John's and Paul's first momentous meeting.

Below: The church continues to serve the religious needs of the area and is a focal point in the neighbourhood.

That century saw a huge increase in the local population and, in 1887, the church that would later allow for John and Paul's first meeting was complete. Its 90-foot bell tower climbs to the clouds on what is Liverpool's highest point, giving those who dare unparalleled views of the city, as well as birds-eye glimpses of neighbouring towns in Lancashire and Cheshire. The church hall in which Paul and Lennon struck up their friendship has been recognised for its importance with a stone plaque. The quaint wooden stage on which the Quarrymen performed that summer evening is now in the safe hands of the Museum of Liverpool, and is deemed to be one of the most special items in their collection. In 2007, a celebration to mark the fifty years since the iconic get together was held in the hall and the surviving members of the original Quarrymen performed for a special 1950s-style dance, reminiscent of the scenes half a century before.

Out in the graveyard in which Eleanor Rigby lies, the final resting place of John's uncle, George Toogood Smith, can also be found. When John's parent's separated when he was a toddler, he was sent to live with his Uncle George and Aunt Mimi. Mimi was a regular member of the St Peter's congregation and it was George who helped encourage his nephew into music with the gift of his very own harmonica. He passed away in 1955 never knowing what greatness John would grow up to achieve.

John Lennon and the Quarrymen photographed on that historic day in 1957.

9. THE CASBAH CLUB

One of the earliest venues to host the boys can be found at No. 8 Hayman's Green in the leafy suburb of West Derby. In the late 1950s this was home to the Best family, headed by matriarch Mona Best. She, her husband Johnny, and their two sons moved into this substantial Victorian house, which had previously been occupied by the local Conservative Club. The property boasted no less than fifteen rooms set over two storeys, along with an attic and a large compartmented cellar. With so much space Mona harboured dreams to open a stylish coffee bar to rival similar establishments around the city, especially that of the Lowlands Youth Club just across the street. Mona's place would be members only with a target market of trendy teenagers – like her eldest son Pete.

Pete was a typical seventeen-year-old, with a liking for rock 'n' roll and dashing good looks. He wasn't too bad on the drums either and played for a band known as the Blackjacks. The neighbouring youth club was not only familiar to the Bests but also to George Harrison. When he wasn't playing alongside Paul and John, George joined in with the Les Stewart Quartet where he manned the guitar gigging in and around West Derby. It was around this time when George began courting his first ever girlfriend, Ruth Morrison, who was well-acquainted with the Best brothers. She suggested that her boyfriend's band should perform on the opening night so George and Les Stewart, along with fellow members Ken Brown and Geoff Skinner, surveyed the old basement, where they were promptly offered a weekly residency if they promised to redecorate the club. The lads got to work and spent several evenings and weekends sprucing up the place in time for the big launch. Unfortunately, the quartet had a huge argument over missing rehearsal time, resulting in its immediate disbandment just days before the launch. Mona was left without a headline act, a half-finished venue, and an urgent need for help. George came to the rescue and said that his friends Paul and John would be happy to step in last minute. They visited the house to speak to Mona and see where they would be performing, but, to the boys' surprise, they were handed paintbrushes and set to work on finishing the decorating. Among other additions, John mistook the can of gloss paint for matt, resulting in the creation of a very slow-drying black ceiling, while in an adjoining space Paul completed a rather vivid array of multi-coloured stripes. The boys were happy to get stuck in and relished the opportunity to leave their mark on this exciting new hang-out.

On the pleasant summer evening of 29 August 1959, the Quarrymen – featuring John, Paul, George and Ken Brown – played to the 300 excited new members who had come to experience the unveiling of the Casbah. After patiently queuing up the driveway and paying an admission fee, access was gained through a door in the garden that led down into the new venue. Mona had only thought up the name a few days earlier, having

A young Paul and John seen performing to the captivated basement crowd.

compared the vast cellar to the walled citadel of Casbah in Algeria. Guests enjoyed soft drinks, coffee, sweets and snacks as well as live music. The boys were paid 15s and shared a single microphone connected to a somewhat basic PA system. From this first night until it closure on 24 June 1962, the teens played the Casbah a total of forty-four times. It was here where the boys learnt the skills that would later catch the eye of Brian Epstein and developed their endearing on-stage chemistry. Pete Best's presence hadn't gone unnoticed in the crowd and by the time the Beatles needed a drummer in 1960, he seemed the perfect man for the job.

No. 8 Hayman's Green is now Grade II listed and remains under the ownership of the Best family. The building is open to visitors who can explore the extraordinary underground performance space set beneath this rambling Victorian residence. 'I think it's a good idea to let people know about the Casbah,' said Paul. 'They know about The Cavern, they know about some of those things, but the Casbah was the place where all that started. We helped paint it and stuff. We looked upon it as our personal club.' Today the historic coffee bar appears just as it did all those years ago and even features original artwork, furniture and fittings from those legendary early appearances.

Above: The converted cellar is still owned by the Best family and is open for tours.

Below: The underground entrance that greets visitors to the Casbah today.

10. YE CRACKE, RICE STREET

Ye Cracke is known to have served some of its earliest beverages in 1825. Back then the pub was called the Ruthin Castle, and had probably been a beerhouse of some description for some years before. It stands alongside an old court dwelling. These were squalid examples of back-to-back housing built around a central courtyard providing the residents living there only sub-standard conditions. The former courtyard now makes up the pub's beer garden, but an original street sign remains standing testament to what once was. This pub stands across the road from the Liverpool Institute and, due to its proximity, the bar was regularly propped up by future Beatles, their friends and acquaintances. It was here where John and Stuart Sutcliffe developed their friendship, and often ordered black velvets at lunchtimes. Their tutor Arthur Ballad was even known to run tutorials in the back room. Ye Crack was most certainly one of John's favourite haunts and it was here where he wooed Cynthia after asking her out to a college dance. On one occasion, John was playing up and was caught lying on the floor in spilt booze mimicking swimming. When a barmaid ordered him up he quickly replied, 'I can't stop, or I'll drown' – words met with drunken laughter from inebriated his friends.

Another less prolific band also came to prominence here – that of the Dissenters. This band consisted of John Lennon, Stuart Sutcliffe and their mutual friends Rod Murray and Bill Harry. The young students had been to listen to a talk by the author and poet Royston Ellis but they were so unimpressed they returned to the pub to berate the evening's events, and decided to put the city on the map themselves. Ultimately, the Dissenters never played a single note, but a long-standing friendship with Ellis prevailed and it is he who was immortalised in the band's 1966 hit 'Paperback Writer'.

This neighbourhood retains much of its historic architecture and atmosphere, sitting within what is known as Liverpool's Georgian Quarter. Stretching from Duke Street in the west over to Grove Street in the east, the Georgian Quarter features splendid examples of grand eighteenth-century housing, built for the most affluent members of Liverpool's merchant classes. Unfortunately, such prosperity never reached Rice Steet, which offers little in the way of significance with the only property of note being the humble Ye Cracke. The pub has changed little since the mid-twentieth century and the visits enjoyed by Lennon and his associates. The interior now features several pieces of Beatles memorabilia, as well as a number of nostalgic sketches of places to be found in the locality. The pub also has an interesting medical connection as it is believed Doctors Thomas C. Gray and John Halton came up with the 'Liverpool Technique' while sitting in the pub during the 1940s. This was a pioneering method of anaesthesia allowing a range of new possibilities in the development of surgery. Their conversations may well have taken place in one of the most

A Mersey Beat era look down Rice Street captures a beer delivery taking place at Ye Cracke.

unusual parts of the building known as the War Office. This is a small snug surrounded by panelled walls where, local legend has it, old soldiers of the Boer War would sit and discuss their memories of the conflict. Nowadays this room – one of the first to be sought by patrons – is certainly one of the more characterful spaces to be found in the whole city.

The historic pub continues to be a popular watering hole for students and Beatles fans.

11. SLATER STREET

This view depicts Slater Street in the heart of Liverpool city centre in the 1960s. Back then Slater Street was home to mix of professions – from wine merchants to electrical engineers – as well as being the address to handful of bars and pubs. It was in 1957 when a young businessman by the name of Allan Williams rented a former watch repair shop at No. 21. His idea was to transform the venue into an exciting new coffee lounge, to be christened the Jacaranda. The name comes from a variety of ornamental flowering tree native to South America. Its colourful petals have given rise to the phrase 'Purple Panic' in university cities where its arrival signals to students that exam season is on the way. Naturally the 'Jac', as it

Slater Street seen in the days when the boys were becoming the most influential band of the era.

became known, was a popular hang-out for students in Liverpool and frequently attracted the likes of John Lennon, Paul McCartney and Stuart Sutcliffe. The coffee shop soon began hosting live music and became a place where wannabe musicians could come and cut their teeth on a public stage. The young trio begged Williams for a chance to play, and in return were put to task on various odd jobs. There was general cleaning and minor repair work, but the most unique task required of the budding band members was the painting of a ladies' room mural by Stuart and John. As the band's popularity grew the boys approached Williams and asked if he would be their manager. Williams had experience in promoting bands and had recently organised a series of gigs in Hamburg for another Liverpool band, Derry and the Seniors. This latest collaboration led to several bookings across Merseyside including Williams' other business, the Blue Angel in nearby Seel Street. These early bookings were not particularly glamorous and the band infamously provided backing music for a local striptease act. In 1960 the group, consisting by then of drummer Pete Best, along with Williams' wife, brother-in law, a translator, and a friend known affectionately as Lord Woodbine, all crammed into Williams' van outside the Jac and headed for a boat to Hamburg. This would be the Beatles' first foreign tour, and one that would show them what life as musicians was really like.

The Jacaranda remains standing on the same Slater Street spot, although its size and décor has changed dramatically through the years. Whatever its appearance may be, the

Today, Slater Street is home to numerous bars and is one of Liverpool's most popular nightspots.

club has most certainly evolved to become a must-see for any Beatles fan and is renowned for being the first commercial venue to ever host the band. However, Allan Williams' time with the band was short-lived. In 1961, he and the boys had a major disagreement over payment, which escalated to such an extent that the parties decided to go their separate ways. Shortly afterwards Williams was contacted by Brian Epstein, who wished to check that the band were free of any contractual obligations. He was advised in no uncertain terms to steer clear of the boys but fortunately for Epstein he paid little attention to the diatribe. What followed was one of the most famous signings in musical history. Williams later wrote a book about his experiences as the band's first manager with the title, *The Man Who Gave Away the Beatles*. He played no part in the boys' subsequent success and is often seen to be one of the industry's most unlucky characters for letting what would go on to become the world's most famous boy band slip through his fingers.

Nowadays the Jacaranda is under new ownership but continues the tradition of encouraging new and emerging talent running open-mic nights for up-and-coming musicians; it even has its own rehearsal space where modern bands can practise in same room where the boys learnt the ropes some fifty years earlier. The Jac has gone back to its roots upstairs, with a coffee shop and vinyl record emporium. The social make-up of Slater Street has also transformed, with many properties also now under new ownership. The old wine and spirit merchants of William Guinan's day has kept its beverage connections having become part of a bar known as the Shipping Forecast. This venue also encompasses the adjacent business, helping to make this part of the city quite the hub for nightlife, along with the nearby O'Briens public house and the eponymous Slaters Bar just across the street. Allan Williams often enjoyed discussing his time working with the band and made countless public appearances right up until his death in 2016.

The celebrated Jacaranda where Allan Williams opened up his new coffee lounge in 1957.

12. SEEL STREET

This quirky street takes its name from the Georgian merchant Thomas Seel, who once lived in a grand mansion built in nearby Hanover Street early in the eighteenth century. It had a long rear garden adjoining what was a rural field stretching out into the distance. It wasn't until around 1790 when the land was divided into plots and a collection of early buildings began to take shape. It is believed that in 1805 Doctor William Henry Duncan, the world's first chief medical officer, was born in the very building that would later become the Wyvern Social Club. By the time Allan Williams had spotted this place in the early 1960s, it had become an empty shell. He made enquiries and sought out a lease for a new nightclub venture, naming it after his favourite Marlene Dietrich film. It was here in the Blue Angel that the Beatles first showed a glimmer of their true potential for stardom. In 1960, Williams had been tasked with finding a suitable backing band for the pop superstar Billy Fury. Fury was what young musicians aspired to be: handsome, rich, famous, and the fact that he was from Liverpool made that dream all the more enticing. Among the acts that morning was John, Paul, George and Stuart Sutcliffe, as well as their temporary drummer Tommy Moore. Together they were the Silver Beatles. The boys wore black shirts with jean-like trousers, giving them what John believed to be a classy touch. Whatever their appearance, the Blue Angel was no palace, and on 10 May the boys performed among the tables and chairs in a tired venue undergoing refurbishment. The audition also had room for improvement, with George recalling the whole affair to be a bit of a shambles. It was Cass and the Casanovas who won the day, but nevertheless the boys had made some sort of impression. Ten days later, Fury's agent rang Williams and asked for a last-minute band for the pop act Johnny Gentle for a short tour of Scotland. As it turned out – with a few white lies to family and teachers and employers – the Silver Beatles would be available. Their ramshackle performance at the old social club had been enough. Later that year, the Blue Angel was also the setting for Pete Best's audition to be the band's new drummer on their upcoming tour of Hamburg. As Best was the only drummer they knew who would be available, his audition there was merely a formality. During their second visit to Germany, Williams famously fell out with the Beatles over certain contractual legalities and banned them from the club. They weren't allowed back to the Blue Angel for months, but from then on it became one of their favourite places to hang out, drink and socialise.

Today, the Blue Angel thrives as a nightclub and the rest of Seel Street continues as a popular place to socialise, with bars and clubs aplenty. Much of the street has changed from its original quaint residential character, although some larger properties here have become student accommodation for Liverpool's thousands of young academics. Seel Street was recently voted as one of the UK's 'hippest' street thanks to its rich array of styles, amenities and of course heritage. The Blue Angel has affectionately become known as the Raz due to

Seel Street seen from the corner of Slater Street in the 1960s.

A comparison view of Seel Street shows the vicinity in more recent times.

The Blue Angel, where the Beatles unsuccessfully auditioned as the backing band for Billy Fury.

its variety of cheap drinks and the subsequent states of drunkenness that inevitably follow. This popularity, however, almost led to its downfall. The club was temporarily silenced in 2008 when the city council stepped in and seized its sound system after complaints from nearby residents living elsewhere in the Ropewalks district of the city. After a lengthy legal battle, it was agreed that the club could not open its patio doors past 7p.m. as to avoid disturbing the apartments in a nearby street. Since then there appears to have been no further problems with drinkers enjoying a happy atmosphere well into the very early hours.

13. LITHERLAND TOWN HALL

The town of Litherland was once a distinct urban district a few miles north of Liverpool. Its town hall provided the boys plenty of opportunities to perform and they are known to have taken to the stage here on at least twenty separate occasions. The phrase 'Beatlemania' has been a part of our common lexicon for years, but the term owes its existence to some ground-breaking renditions almost six decades ago. In the winter of 1960, music promoter Bob Wooler was introduced to the band through their manager Allan Williams. All but one was back from their first tour of Germany when Wooler secured the boys a gig in Litherland. Nineteen-year-old bassist Chas Newby stepped in for Stuart Sutcliffe, who had stayed behind on the Continent. Understandably, this particular booking had something of a European allure to it, with 'Direct from Hamburg' featuring all over the night's promotional material. Of course, they were Scousers through and through, but the crowd didn't realise and many remarked upon how well they sang in English. The boys' time abroad had ended in a rather embarrassing deportation, but their ability to play and overall stage presence had greatly improved. Their performance on the evening of 27 December 1960 would confirm their status as one of Liverpool's hottest acts. John later recalled how Hamburg had changed them and that there was now a real difference between his group and all the other acts out there. He was right. The crowd was cheering in a way they never had before. Their opening song of 'Long Tall Sally' had the entire room screaming and there was a spontaneous surge towards the front of the stage. The audience didn't dance as expected, but stood – a sea of enamoured faces looking up fixated on the band's every move. The Beatles were truly something else! After that night, the boys were immediately scheduled for more shows across the city and paid a decent rate. Future appearances at Litherland Town Hall would see the boys share the stage with the likes of Gerry and the Pacemakers, who even joined the lads on stage for a special and drunken one-off amalgamation as the Beatmakers.

Litherland now falls under the borough of Sefton and as such its town hall no longer serves any political purpose. Instead the hall has been converted into a NHS centre through a refurbishment that has significantly altered the look and layout of the building. Despite being the epicentre of Beatlemania, a force that spread around the world with seemingly endless momentum, the building bears no marker or indication that this was where the trailblazing craze all began. In 2009, Beatles fan Colin Unwin proposed the installation of a plaque celebrating the centre's connections with the band, and even sold his prized 1965 acoustic guitar to personally pay for it. Health bosses put a stop to the idea, stating that an increase in tourism would potentially affect staff and their ability to carry out their duties. However, officials have noted that they recognised the importance of the building's heritage and chose to retain rather than demolish the old town hall during its redevelopment.

Above: Screaming fans in Litherland Town Hall brought about the birth of Beatlemania in December 1960.

Below: The former town hall now serves the local community as a centre for the NHS.

The Beatles' final appearance at Litherland Town Hall took place on the evening of 9 November 1961. This was their second gig of the day, having first performed at the Cavern Club in the afternoon, where they had wowed an excitable lunchtime crowd, including Brian Epstein. He had popped by to see the new local sensation he had heard so much about. After helping out on a few occasions during college half term, Chas Newby was asked to stay on with the band but declined, wishing to return his studies to become a teacher of mathematics. He didn't think the boys would get anywhere with their music, and it would be another two years before their first single of 'Love Me Do' would finally be released.

The poster that advertised the Beatles' momentous gig at Litherland Town Hall.

14. MATHEW STREET

The spiritual home of the Beatles has to be Mathew Street. This narrow, winding passage, nestled between a neighbourhood of old Victorian warehouses, has become eternally entwined within the legacy of the band thanks to the opening of a certain subterranean venue. The Cavern Club opened as a jazz club on 16 January 1957 – well before the billing of the boys. In those days, the owner was the fresh-faced entrepreneur Alan Sytner. Liverpool born, he had enjoyed the atmosphere of Paris nightlife, and as a teenager could be found soaking up the bohemian atmosphere in the capital's club scene. In particular, his experience of De La Huchette in the Latin Quarter spurred within him a passion to recreate the Parisian club back home. When the opportunity came to buy the city cellar located at No. 10 with the help of his father, Alan leapt at the opportunity. Unusually, he chose not to have an alcohol licence, but he would know the clientele were truly there for the music. The late January opening was unfortunate as the profitable Christmas festivities had already been and gone. When the Cavern opened with the Merseysippi Jazz Band, the Wall City Jazzmen, the Ralph Watmough Jazz Band and the Coney Island Skiffle Group, the line-up attracted over 2,000 people. The venue could only fit 600, but despite having to turn many away Sytner was thrilled to know he had created an instant hit. He insisted on a fine balance between jazz and skiffle, but the emerging trend for rock 'n' roll was banned. When the Quarrymen played here and tried to play a few more edgy songs, they were handed a note to swiftly cut it out. Two years after opening, it became apparent that the Cavern Club was in need of urgent works to its ventilation system, but these were improvements that Alan just could not afford. Auditor Ray McFall stepped in to take over the ownership of the venue and immediately pushed for more popular rock 'n' roll acts to turn the place around. The Beatles played their first lunchtime booking on 9 February 1961. That Thursday gig, for which the band was paid just £5, would be the beginning of a whole new era of world-changing music.

Mathew Street has a long and interesting heritage and was founded long before the days of the Fab Four. During the city's early years, this part of Liverpool was largely agricultural, and devoid of the tall warehouses and industrial constructions we see today. As Liverpool grew in power and importance the land around this lively port became a valuable commodity. This fact was not lost upon Mr Mathew Pluckington, who secured a large plot not too distant to the thriving waterfront. His purchase later became known as Pluckington's Alley and by the mid-eighteenth century it was home to a horde of traders and residents. Through the decades, this little nondescript alley developed into substantial proportions and was populated by multistorey warehouses packed high with produce imported off ships from all over the world. In time, the passageway shook off its vernacular

Liverpool's famous Mathew Street where the Beatles played regularly in the subterranean Cavern Club.

Mathew Street is one of the city's most popular attractions, welcoming thousands every year. The original entrance to the Cavern has been memorialised within the modern development.

moniker and was renamed in honour of the original landlord – spelling included. It wasn't until the mid-twentieth century with the arrival of the revolutionary sound of Mersey Beat that Mathew Street became a die-hard destination of musical pilgrimage. It is difficult to imagine just how this uneven rural track in a quiet fishing village transformed into one of the planet's most famous and must-see locations. The Saturday of 3 August 1963 marked the last of 292 performances at the Cavern Club by the Beatles, which had gained legendary status for fans, bands and recording artists across the world. Despite this acclaim, British Rail took over the ownership of the building in 1972. They wished to clear away this section of the street for a new ventilation shaft serving the city's expanding underground railway network. The following year bulldozers moved in to raze the buildings at street level and the original cellar was filled in with the rubble. In the end, the proposed ventilation shaft was never built, and it took a decade for the idea to bring the Cavern back to life to be seriously considered. Structural issues meant that the original cellar itself could never be resurrected, but 15,000 bricks from the original site were used in the authentic reconstruction of the new Cavern Club just a few feet away.

15. NEMS OF WHITECHAPEL

The chain North End Music Store (NEMS) was owned by Harry and Malka Epstein. They had taken over the running of the successful family business, Epstein & Sons, successfully retailing in household furniture. Harry spotted a gap in the market for the sale of musical instruments, so, after careful planning, their shop at Walton Road expanded and NEMS was formally established. Their son Brian had shown a flare for sales but his real ambitions lay in entertainment. After an unsuccessful attempt to be a London actor in the early 1950s, Brian returned home to Liverpool where he was put in charge of the Great Charlotte Street branch of NEMS. He improved the range to include records, which proved a big hit with customers, and business boomed. A new branch opened at Nos 12–14 Whitechapel with a policy that the company would stock any record that was commercially available. Legend has it that on the afternoon of 28 October 1961, teenager Raymond Jones entered the store and requested 'My Bonnie', a little-known track recorded in Germany featuring a band called the Beatles. None of the clerks – nor Brian Epstein – had ever heard of them, but they promised to do their best to get the single in stock. It appears that Brian should at least have had an awareness of the band as they appeared on the front cover of *Mersey Beat*, a local music periodical to which Epstein regularly contributed. Whatever the case, the Whitechapel branch of NEMS was less than a five-minute walk from Mathew Street, so on 9 November Brian and his assistant arrived at the Cavern to see one of the Beatles' lunchtime sessions. He would later say how enamoured he was by their performance. 'I was immediately struck by their music, their beat, and their sense of humour on stage. And even afterwards when I met them I was struck again by their personal charm. And it was there that really it all started.' Given his later success, it is all the more remarkable that up until this point Brian had no experience with managing bands, but merely held a wish to try his hand at the entertainment business. After several meetings with the boys at his office, it was agreed that Brian would officially manage the band and a life-changing contract was formally drafted.

Today, gone is the imposing structure that housed NEMS for several decades and instead in its place is a rather large branch of the American clothing store Forever 21. The original building that housed the humble beginnings of Epstein's empire was torn down in 2012 after being deemed unsuitable for modern day commercial tenants. It had been described as the most important site in music history, but this sadly did not warrant any legal protect from the authorities. It was from this site that Epstein negotiated the Beatles' first recording contract using his charm and connections in the music industry to open doors that may have otherwise remained shut. Six months after teaming up with their new manager the boys were able to sign for Parlophone, one of EMI's smaller labels headed by George Martin. It was however Brian's enthusiasm and personal belief in the band that

The Beatles' manager Brian Epstein had his office here at NEMS in the Whitechapel area of Liverpool.

ultimately persuaded the firm to give them a chance. The band returned to the NEMS store in 1963 for a public appearance promoting their new single, 'Please Please Me', and gave a special acoustic performance at the foot of the staircase to Brian's office. The boys stayed to sign copies of their new track to crowds of adoring fans who jostled into the modest Whitechapel shop. As their fame grew, NEMS Enterprises (the management company Brian had set up to deal with his music promotions) had outgrown its original office and was forced to move to a new location in nearby Moorfields, taking on a new office manager, errand boys, two telephonists and even a press officer to deal with the overwhelming levels of enquiries about the band. With their fame growing at an expediential rate, NEMS Enterprises was again required to move, this time to London to an address in Monmouth Street in the centre of the capital. In 2010 Cilla Black, arguably Epstein's second most famous signing, unveiled a plaque honouring her former manager and the work of NEMS Enterprises. As of yet, no such plaque can be found in Liverpool's Whitechapel.

The view has changed considerably since the days of the Fab Four.

16. NEW BRIGHTON TOWER BALLROOM

New Brighton can be found on the shores of the Wirral peninsula and was once one of the UK's favourite holiday resorts. New Brighton's history as a destination begins in the 1830s when businessman James Atherton purchased land here with a view of emulating the great Regency playground of Brighton on the south coast of Britain. Until then the most significant building to be constructed here was a defensive battery known as Fort Perch Rock in 1826. This acted as a military outpost overlooking Liverpool Bay and the entrance to the wealthy port. After Atherton's intervention, large villas with unparalleled sea views began to be built on the coastal cliffs, with hotels, shops and public houses quickly following. Throughout the nineteenth century New Brighton had become a real tourist magnet, but popular with mostly working classes rather than the more well-to-do patrons Atherton had earlier hoped for. In 1900, the resort cemented its name into the history books with the official opening of the country's tallest structure. This was New Brighton Tower, a steel triumph that stood at 567 feet high, topped off by an observation deck. On the ground was the UK's largest provincial theatre capable of seating 2,500 people. There was also the Tower Ballroom, which boasted a sprung dance floor enjoyed by up to 1,000 swaying couples at a time, as well as room for live bands and spectators. Unfortunately, the super structure proved too costly to maintain throughout the First World War, so in 1919 the decision was taken to dismantle the Tower and sell the metal for scrap. The brick base that contained the ballroom, however, remained, and between 1961 and 1963 the Beatles played here live on twenty-seven occasions, more than any other venue except the Cavern Club. Their first appearance was part of promoter Sam Leach's big musical extravaganza he called Operation Big Beat, on 10 November 1961. They appeared alongside Rory Storm and the Hurricanes, Gerry and the Pacemakers, the Remo Four, and Kingsize Taylor and the Dominoes in a mammoth gig billed from 7.30 p.m. right through to 1.30 a.m. The night would be a test of the boys' logistics and time management. They eventually kicked off the night with their first set at around 8 p.m., then sped off through the Mersey Tunnel to make a second booking in Knotty Ash, over 10 miles away. They were due back at the Tower again at 11 p.m. to play once more to the estimated 3,000 attendees who had packed out the historic seaside venue. Two weeks later on 24 November the boys played here again, this time to no less than 4,500 people – setting their own UK mainland attendance record. Their final performance at New Brighton's Tower Ballroom occurred on 14 June 1963. It was bittersweet for twenty-one-year-old Paul who was caught speeding (again) on his way home from the gig in Seabank Road. He appeared before magistrates who handed him a twelve-month driving ban and a fine.

It was in the early hours of Saturday 5 April 1969 when reports that the Tower Ballroom was on fire reached the local brigade. On the previous evening, staff had conducted their

A mid-twentieth-century photograph of New Brighton showing the record-breaking Tower Ballroom.

routine checks and found nothing amiss. However, they failed to inspect the area closest to the stage and it was here where experts believed the blaze to have originated. By the time firefighters arrived – just after 5 a.m. – huge plumes of smoke were pouring from the blackened windows and parts of the building were already beginning to buckle. In moments, a wall to the main ballroom caved in, allowing the flames to take hold and spread even further around the venue. To make matters worse, the nearby boating lake had recently been drained, forcing the brigade to source water from the marine lake further down the road. By 7 a.m., twenty-five pumps manned by 150 firemen were tackling the blaze, with many more racing to assist from neighbouring authorities. As daybreak came, it became apparent that the Tower Ballroom could not be saved and the heartbreaking decision was taken to let the building go. Its stage had played host to not only the Beatles but other big names, such as Jerry Lee Lewis, Little Richard and the Rolling Stones. That night one of Merseyside's most iconic performance spaces was destroyed, bringing to an end decades of irreplaceable musical history. In time the site of the Tower was cleared and the land used for residential housing. The Victorian pier from which the original photograph was taken was dismantled in 1977 in a further blow to the town's heritage. The rise in affordable foreign holidays saw New Brighton's appeal as a destination diminish and the resort's Golden Age came to an end. In recent times, the town's fortunes have significantly improved with substantial investment and improvement works taking place. The £60 million regeneration scheme at New Brighton has been the largest Wirral has ever seen, bringing a new cinema, hotel, casino, restaurants and bars to the seafront, along with thousands of new visitors.

Above: The old performance venue was destroyed during a fire in 1969 after nearly seventy years of entertainment.

Below: A plaque now commemorates the Beatles' New Brighton Tower Ballroom performances.

THE BEATLES
Played at the
Tower Ballroom,
New Brighton
on 27 occasions

1961 - 1963

17. THE LIVERPOOL EMPIRE

Located in Lime Street, the Empire Theatre has been a leading light in the world of Liverpool entertainment for decades. There has been a stage on this site ever since the Prince of Wales Theatre and Opera House opened its doors for the first time in the winter of 1866 with a performance of the opera *Faust*. Back then this was the city's largest theatre, designed in a classical style and handsomely fitted and decorated with a host of fine and intricate features. Stage machinery was powered by means of steam and beautiful gas lights were used to provide illumination. Within a year the theatre was renamed in honour of the Princess of Wales and became known as the Royal Alexandra Theatre and Opera House. By the closing years of the century the venue was suffering under serious financial strain. The theatre and musical hall chain of Moss Empires stepped in and brought the venue, changing its name once again, this time branded to the Empire. The firm had the building refurbished by specialist theatre architect Frank Matcham and continued to run it in a similar style, opening with the pantomime *Cinderella* and also producing a selection of variety shows. Thirty years later a new Empire, bigger and better than before, opened to eager audiences on 9 March 1925. Constructed with a steel frame and a mix of brick and Portland stone, the new theatre was fashioned in a free neoclassical design, including a set of robust ionic columns fronting the façade. The building boasted almost 2,500 seats, making this theatre the largest two-tier theatre in the country and it had the largest auditorium in Europe at the time. Many famous performers have graced its stage over the years, included Bing Crosby, Laurel and Hardy, Julie Andrews and Frank Sinatra to name but a few. Although the Quarrymen had performed at the venue several times in the late 1950s, it wasn't until October 1962 that the Beatles first appeared at the Empire. The band took second billing to Little Richard with support from Craig Douglas, Kenny Lynch, the Breakaways and Sounds Incorporated. Over the years the band were booked over ten times, and had some particularly notable performances. In December 1963, a special concert for members of their Northern Arena Fan Club was organised, along with filming for an episode of *Juke Box Jury* at the nearby Odeon Cinema. The band's final concert in their hometown took place at the Empire in 1965 as part of a UK tour to coincide with the release of the studio album *Rubber Soul*. Over 40,000 fans applied for tickets and many were left disappointed at missing out on seeing the band play hits such as 'I feel Fine', 'Help!' and 'We Can Work It Out'.

George Harrison was the first to make a reappearance at the Empire in 1969 with the American musical duo Delaney & Bonnie, but this was to be his last ever live performance in his home city. Promoting their album *Red Rose Speedway* as well as the single 'Live and Let Die', Paul McCartney played the Empire in 1973 with his band Wings, returning once again in 1975 with Wings' 'Over the World' tour. The latter performance also featured some

The acclaimed Liverpool Empire. A theatre has stood here in Lime Street since Victorian times.

of McCartney's compositions from the Beatles era, such as 'Yesterday', 'Lady Madonna' and 'The Long and Winding Road'. Their inclusion proved especially popular and marked the first time that McCartney had performed material from the Beatles' repertoire since their break-up in 1970. Throughout that decade the Empire fell into a period of decline, as the theatre competed with the unstoppable rise of home television and other forms of entertainment. The company began to accrue unaffordable debts and the venue was reluctantly put up for sale. Its prominent position next to Lime Street railway station and standing on one of Liverpool's main traffic routes made the building very desirable for a car park, and it came very close to being reduced to tarmac. Fortunately, a rescue package was established that saw ownership of the theatre transfer to Merseyside County Council. Popular shows from the West End helped trigger a resurgence in theatre and the Empire experienced something of a renaissance of its own. This boost in popularity coincided with a change in local government and the establishment of Liverpool City Council. Council members wished to discharge their responsibility of the Empire to a private enterprise that saw Apollo Leisure take over the running of the venue along with a board of trustees. An extensive programme of refurbishments were carried out to fix the increasingly tired looking building, and the theatre was lovingly restored to its former glory. In 1992, Ringo Starr appeared with his All Starr Band, with his son Zak on the drums. The performance

The Beatles first played at the Liverpool Empire in 1962 supporting American singer-songwriter Little Richard.

was the centrepiece of the Disney Channel's *Ringo: Going Home* special, which featured Ringo taking his son Jason on a walking tour of his old Liverpool haunts, peppered with footage and songs from his night at the Empire. This was the final occasion a Beatle ever performed at the venue. Today the Liverpool Empire continues to serve entertainment-seekers far and wide with a busy calendar of shows and performances.

18. MOUNT PLEASANT

This is the view that greeted the pedestrians of Mount Pleasant in the 1960s. In the eighteenth century this neighbourhood was renowned for its proximity to the beautiful pleasure gardens of Ranelagh Place, and as a result large mansions began to emerge for the well-to-do. This area also featured a famous bowling green that served not only as an excellent venue for the sport, but also acted as the ideal meeting place for a great many rendezvous. Mount Pleasant was mentioned as early as 1687 as a place of popularity and

How Mount Peasant would have appeared to John and Cynthia after their wedding on 23 August 1962.

has remained adorned with a multitude of handsome Georgian properties. It was on this stretch of road on 23 August 1962 that John Lennon and his pregnant girlfriend Cynthia Powell married in a civil ceremony at the local registry office, located within an eighteenth-century townhouse at No. 64. It was thought that knowledge of John's nuptials would affect the band's marketing appeal, so the marriage was kept secret from the press. It was to be a rather modest affair, with the bride's brother Tony, his wife Marjorie, George Harrison, Paul McCartney and Brian Epstein being the only guests. The day did not go to plan, with most of the ceremony drowned out by the noise of buildings works in the property next door. Cynthia wore a second-hand dress as they were too poor to afford a proper wedding outfit. With vows exchanged and the formalities eventually complete, the party headed out into the pouring rain and over to Recce's café a short walk down the hill in Clayton Square, where guests had something of a non-traditional wedding meal of soup, chicken and trifle. Both the registry office and Reece's restaurant had played host to John's own parents' wedding some twenty-four years earlier. For the start of John and Cynthia's married life together there was to be no honeymoon or indeed wedding night as the band had been booked to play in Chester later that evening with a host of other performances scheduled for the year ahead.

Liverpool's registry office has since moved to the esteemed confines of St George's Hall, where couples can marry in either the wooden-panelled Grand Jury room or the Sefton Room, overlooking St John's Gardens. The old registry office of John and Cynthia's time remains standing and has been recognised for its historic and architectural importance. Mount Pleasant has undergone significant scenes of change throughout the years, with

Sadly many of the older buildings in this locality have since vanished from the cityscape.

a number of properties on this part of the street lost to more modern development. To the left of the image stands Roscoe Gardens, named in honour of one of Liverpool's most important figures, William Roscoe. Born in 1753 at an inn on Mount Pleasant, Roscoe was an avid historian, leading abolitionist, art collector, MP, lawyer, banker, botanist and writer. His influence throughout the city remains to this day, with his name frequently referenced in a number of city roads, pubs and institutions. Across the way, the historic structures that would have overlooked the Lennons as they hurried to their wedding meal have disappeared. Casualties have included the Mount Pleasant Wesleyan Chapel, which later became the Mardi Bras Club. This was a popular venue on Liverpool's music circuit in the 1960s and was one of the many local stages the Beatles played on their journey to international stardom. The gigantic pillar piecing the sky is St Johns Beacon and was erected in 1969 as a revolving restaurant, with diners enjoying stunning views with each course. It has become home to several radio stations but, alas, can no longer rotate.

No. 64, the site of the registry office where John and Cynthia were wed.

19. HULME HALL, PORT SUNLIGHT

Port Sunlight sits across the waters of the Mersey on the Wirral peninsula and was the setting for the birth of the Beatles as we know them. The picturesque village was founded in 1888 by the soap entrepreneur William Hesketh Lever. Before the arrival of the Levers this part of the country consisted of little more than marshy flatlands. The location and conditions were good enough for Lever, who wished to move his Warrington soapworks to a large plot close to the river and railway. As well as the factory, he envisioned a whole purpose-built village dedicated entirely to the wellbeing of his workforce. Second to business was his love of architecture, and during building works he collaborated closely with designers to achieve beautiful and unique examples of domestic dwellings, commercial enterprises and leisure facilities. One such creation was Hulme Hall, which was erected in 1901 as a women's dining hall. A decade later this became an art gallery, which housed some of the then Viscount Leverhulme's vast collection. Half a century later, on the Saturday night of 18 August 1962, it was the Beatles who came to Hulme Hall to perform

Hulme Hall, where Ringo Starr first played as an official member of the band.

with their new drummer Ringo Starr. The Horticultural Society's Annual Show had taken place earlier in the day and, as was customary, the evening would be concluded with a night of live entertainment. The dance was sold out, and over 400 people packed onto the dancefloor. With fan-favourite Pete Best sacked, the boys were unsure as to how his new replacement would be received. Ringo had performed as a stand-in drummer with the boys on several occasions before, but now he was official. Now he was a Beatle. By the end of their hour-long set the boys realised that they had nothing to worry about. Their music sounded different, better somehow. The Fab Four had finally found their perfect line-up.

After Ringo's debut, the band returned to Hulme Hall to play again the following October, when they also gave their first ever broadcast interview over the airwaves of the nearby hospital station Radio Clatterbridge. The boys answered questions in a makeshift studio, which, in reality, was just a small space next to the male toilets. During the interview, throughout which all four members wore impeccable Birkenhead-sourced Beno Dorn suits, Paul confirmed that John was the leader of the group after interviewer Monty Lister suggested George was in charge due to his role on lead guitar.

Given the social significance of Port Sunlight as a centre of Victorian industry and model village, much of the neighbourhood remains just as it did when the Beatles played here all those decades ago. The hall is still used as an event space for all kinds of occasions from weddings to beer festivals, antique fairs and corporate parties. Until the 1980s the properties here were reserved solely for the staff of Unilever and their families, but in recent years these houses have become quite sought after for their chocolate-box appearance

Port Sunlight retains much of its original character with many listed buildings to be found here.

and historic features. There are nearly 200 listed buildings within the village boundaries, including the exquisite war memorial in the centre of the village, which was designed by W. Goscombe John. In its centre is a cross on a plinth, both in granite, surrounded by eleven bronze figures. Upon the plinth are a series of plaques containing the names of employees of Lever Brothers who were lost in the World Wars. This memorial is Grade-I listed, making it one of the most important structures in the entire country. Port Sunlight also boasts its own museum dedicated to telling the story of the village, which features a special exhibition to the Beatles and their long-standing connections to the Wirral.

The Beatles take part in their first ever broadcast interview to Radio Clatterbridge.

20. THE MAJESTIC, CONWAY STREET

The town of Birkenhead is often overshadowed by her big sister Liverpool, but situated just over the water on the opposite side of the River Mersey, this town has a long and fascinating heritage all of its own. Birkenhead is home to the oldest standing building in the whole of Merseyside, the Priory. This has stood on the banks of the river since 1150. It was the monks here who originally petitioned King Edward for transportation rights in the fourteenth century, thus creating that very first ferry across the Mersey, made famous across the world during the Mersey Beat era. What would become the Majestic Ballroom in Conway Street opened in 1916, but previously the building had been Birkenhead's General Post Office since mid-Victorian times. In 1900, this unassuming property made headlines for playing host to the brutal killing of caretaker George Fell. His death, along with the theft of £142 17s 8d remains one of Merseyside's longest and most mysterious unsolved murders. The building became the Birkenhead Super in 1924 before finally becoming the Majestic in 1962. The Beatles first performed here on 28 June 1962, and went on to make a further sixteen appearances. It was not uncommon to see hundreds of fans queuing around

A very early view of Birkenhead's Conway Street, which later housed the Majestic Ballroom.

the block waiting for tickets, with many left out in the cold due to the boys' overwhelming popularity. The December of that year saw not only the band play a conventional evening gig, but also take part in the midnight Mersey Beat Poll Awards. They won for the second year in a row, thrashing Lee Curtis and the All Stars into second place, along with their new drummer Pete Best. The Beatles triumphantly closed the show at 4 a.m., carefully avoiding their recently dismissed bandmate whom Brian had been asked to let go just a few months earlier.

This modern depiction of Conway Street shows how the Majestic and its surroundings have changed considerably since its former life as a post office. The building's façade has become more elaborate with influences of classical design roughly incorporated into its frontage. The neighbouring funeral directors of old is now a nightclub and the large red-brick building nearby, once an Edwardian school, is now known as the Conway Centre and provides council services. The Majestic is no longer an entertainment venue, having closed its doors in 1969. Afterwards it seems to have become a warehouse for furniture storage for a short time before shutting down completely and falling into a sad state of dereliction by the end of the 1960s. The Beatles last played here on 10 April 1963 and today it is a Chinese restaurant. Overall the establishment gives little away as to its former incarnation, but, on looking closely, its frontage does feature a small plaque detailing the building's musical links to the world's most famous boy band and its past use as one of Merseyside's most popular dance halls.

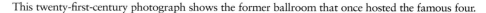

This twenty-first-century photograph shows the former ballroom that once hosted the famous four.

21. HIGH STREET

Prior to the premiere of the band's first feature film, *A Hard Day's Night,* on 10 July 1964, the boys attended a civic reception at Liverpool Town Hall. That afternoon the roads around the hall became awash with screaming fans, many having been waiting since early morning. Their presence caused never before seen scenes of mayhem, with thousands filling doorways, pavements and even shop windows, all eager to catch a glimpse of their musical idols. For some the excitement was too much and it was reported that nearly 400 teenage girls fainted. Some had to be lifted over the crowds and passed forwards to medics unable to breach the throng of people. Scores of wooden stretchers lay around the building as a team of ambulance staff ferried comatose bodies to makeshift recovery zones. Ambulances ran a shuttle service to hospitals, with many patients complaining of breathlessness and crushed ribs. One woman became so ill she was given artificial respiration at the roadside. The screaming fans battled with 1,000 constables, including members of the mounted section, who struggled to control the crowds as Castle Street was brought to a standstill. At 6.55 p.m. John, Paul, George and Ringo arrived in a limousine waving in such a style befitting the most spectacular of royal visits. Guests that evening included the boys' friends and families, the Bishop of Liverpool, Lord and Lady Derby, Bessie Braddock MP and other local dignitaries. After the meal the band were invited out to witness the deafening screams of their admiring public from the balcony. A sea of fluttering Union Jack flags waved behind a wall of arm-in-arm policemen who fought to keep the fans at bay. Chief Constable Joseph Smith remarked that he had not seen anything like it since Everton won the cup in 1934. Back inside, Lord Mayor Louis Caplan gave a speech to the assembled audience in the magnificent ballroom, along with the presentation of city keys – one for each of the boys. The Beatles had officially been bestowed the freedom of the city and by 9 p.m. the band had left for the short trip to the Odeon Cinema for the first northern showing of their new film. Once again, their arrival was met by thousands of screaming fans.

This small side street adjacent to the Town Hall is one of the oldest in Liverpool. Today it is known as High Street, a somewhat small and unremarkable route connecting Dale Street and Exchange Flags. Evidence of the street's more hazardous past can be seen in the wall where several instances of shrapnel damage blemishes the stonework. Up ahead, Castle Street retains much of its Victorian splendour and looks remarkably comparable to the evening of the premier. The red-brick property in the distance was built in 1877 for the picture dealers Agnews and used as a shop and art gallery, but by the 1960s it had become a branch of the Midland Bank. Adjacent is the striking silver structure that the Midland Bank had commissioned in 1967, opening its doors four years later. Its unusual form warranted the building to be granted listed status as an outstanding example of pop architecture, built to engage the young and vibrant consumers of the era. In years gone by, this location

Medical staff struggle to help exhausted fans in chaotic scenes outside Liverpool Town Hall in 1964.

The same scene today shows little change to this small historic side street.

was of distinct importance lying at the heart of an emerging maritime metropolis. It was then known as Juggler Street, one of but a few streets to be found around these parts. In 1207, King John granted this small coastal conurbation a charter recognising all the liberties and customs of its people. It was then that Liverpool began to formally develop with Juggler Street recognised as one of the city's original seven streets. It is believed that it derived its name from the numerous jugglers and performers who used to entertain people around here in medieval times. Records indicate that there had once been a High Cross positioned at the southern end of the street, with a corresponding White Cross at the other. These markers served as local landmarks and provided a place for traders to ply their wares to the modest population of no more than 1,000 inhabitants at that time.

22. ODEON CINEMA

This scene depicts the much-anticipated arrival of the band at Liverpool Odeon Cinema on 10 July 1964. This was the Northern premiere of boys' critically acclaimed film *A Hard Day's Night*, which had its world premiere four days earlier at London's Pavilion Theatre. This was to be the band's first visit back to Liverpool for some time, and there was concern as to how the so-called prodigal sons would be received. The streets around the cinema were packed with screaming fans, creating what Paul would later describe as, 'the most ridiculous reception we ever had!' In fact, 200,000 people lined the route of the boy's motorcade as they made their way to the London Road venue for the 9 p.m. showing. Police were forced to hold back hordes of admirers and stood arm-in-arm as the mounted police and motorcycle officers cleared a path through the city. The Odeon began life as the Paramount and opened on 15 October 1934 as the largest picture house on Merseyside with its full stage, a Compton organ and 2,670 seats. It had been designed in an art deco style and was the most pre-eminent picture house Liverpool had to offer. The Paramount had been built on the site of an old boxing stadium that had staged bouts at this location since 1911, but this was forced to make way for the rising popularity of moving pictures after two decades of pugilism. The cinema's arrival caused a stir with picture houses already operating in the vicinity including the nearby Scala, Futurist, and Palace De Lux, who complained that another chain, with its own ability for production and distribution, would seriously jeopardise any chance of competition. Nevertheless, the new cinema was permitted and the Paramount served the people of Liverpool and beyond throughout the 1930s. In 1942, Odeon took over the running of the cinema, but in time much of the building's decorative features were altered or completely lost as the cinema transformed to suit modern audiences. Major changes took place throughout the 1960s with a change of layout resulting in an additional screen, and further alterations in subsequent years. The Beatles only played at the Odeon once, in the August of 1963, with a ten-song set. The cinema closed its doors for the final time on 30 September 2008 and was replaced the following day with a purpose-built fourteen-screen Odeon multiplex in the Liverpool One shopping centre.

It is with some irony that the Odeon was relocated to Liverpool's newest shopping destination. London Road had been one of the city's busiest commercial districts for generations, with department stores such as T. J. Hughes, Woolworths, numerous fruit and veg markets and various other offerings to be found in abundance. Changes in buying habits combined with new stores opening elsewhere has seen London Road lose its appeal as a place to shop, but some surviving retailers do remain in what is now a dimming shadow of the neighbourhood's former self. One of twenty-first-century Liverpool's chief commodity is student accommodation. The city now houses over 70,000 students from

The Northern premiere of *A Hard Day's Night* at the Liverpool Odeon on 10 July 1964.

several different universities and is seen as a popular place to work and play. The old Odeon building has given way to Liverpool's new academic appeal and is now the future site of student lettings. When complete, this new construction will give this section of the street a very modern appearance, quite different from its nineteenth and twentieth century neighbours. Its position at the corner of London Road and Pudsey Street makes this address ideally suited for getting to classes as well as exploring all the sights and sounds this exciting city has to offer.

The cinema has reopened in Liverpool One, and this site is now destined to become student accommodation.

23. STRAWBERRY FIELD

In 1967, the Beatles released their double A-side 'Penny Lane'/'Strawberry Fields Forever'. It was written by John Lennon and is viewed as a nostalgic look back at the band's Liverpool origins and his own artistic expression. This combination release broke the band's four-year run of chart-topping releases, reaching No. 2 in the UK singles chart. Despite this, Lennon considered this to be his greatest accomplishment with the Beatles. The track takes its name from a children's home run by the Salvation Army, which had been established just a short walk away from John's home of Mendips in Menlove Avenue. In the summer months, John's aunt Mimi would take him to the garden parties held at the grand Gothic property when the distinctive musical sounds of the Salvation Army's brass band could be heard across the neighbourhood. At other times, John's presence was less welcome, such as

The eminent gates to Strawberry Field Children's Home, which inspired the band's nostalgic 1967 hit.

when he would play in the wooded grounds of the house by scaling over the boundary wall with his mates. This was much to the annoyance of the watchman, who frequently forced the lads to scarper. The verse in the song, 'And nothing to get hung about', is said to be a reference to Lennon's retort, 'they can't hang you for it,' to Mimi's admonishments about playing on the property. These wistful childhood hijinks undoubtedly left their mark on Lennon's memory and helped bring about a song producer George Martin once described as a hazy, impressionistic dreamworld.

Strawberry Field itself only became a children's home in 1936. The house had originally been a vast Victorian mansion set in extensive grounds and home to wealthy shipping magnate George Warren. In later years the property passed into the hands of another maritime merchant, Alexander C. Mitchell, who remained here until his death in 1927. His widow sold the estate to the Salvation Army, who then converted it into rooms to accommodate up to forty disadvantaged children. The building featured a long leafy drive to the main entrance, which was situated behind a large pair of ornate wrought-iron gates. These gates along with their adjoining duo of imposing sandstone pillars have become targets for signatures from Beatles fans the world over, all eager to leave their own mark on the place that inspired one of the band's most classic recordings

By the time the 1970s came around, Strawberry Field had fell into disuse. The building was not properly cared for and had succumbed to rot and decay throughout. Eventually, the building was demolished and the huge Gothic mansion was no more. Parts of the estate were sold off and the money raised helped bring about the construction of new and modern

The entrance to the Strawberry Field is frequently besieged by fans from across the globe.

facilities on the site, including John Lennon Court. This new annex was partly funded by a very generous donation by the Beatle himself. John also left a sum of money to the charity in his will, and Yoko Ono has also contributed to the building's continued use over the years, even taking their son Sean on a visit here in 1984.

In 2000, Strawberry Field fell victim to thieves who had the audacity to cut its famous gates right from their hinges. Children playing nearby told police they had seen two men put the 8-foot-high gates into a blue transit van and drive away. The gates had been an iconic part of Strawberry Field, having stood for at least a century, so it was a huge relief to all when an eagle-eyed scrap dealer informed police after he had recently purchased them in good faith and wished to return the gates to their rightful owner. This incident was enough to put Beatles devotees and heritage experts on edge, and it was agreed that the original gates should be secured safely in storage and that accurate replicas would be installed in their place. Strawberry Field home however did not last forever and in 2005 it was announced that the institution would no longer be operating as an orphanage. Housing children in such places was no longer deemed appropriate and the few remaining orphans left with the charity were found foster families. The site remains empty, but plans have recently been submitted to turn Strawberry Field into a training centre for young adults with learning difficulties, as well as a visitor centre and exhibition centre dedicated to the location's illustrious musical past.

The children's home was once a stately private residence set within its own extensive grounds.

24. PENNY LANE

This road was made famous through the eponymous 1967 single from the Sgt. Pepper sessions, penned largely by Paul McCartney. 'Penny Lane' was derived from a real street well remembered from the band's childhood days. This view depicts Penny Lane from the junction of Dovedale Road. Penny Lane is believed to have been named after the eighteenth-century merchant James Penny, a staunch proponent of the transatlantic slave trade on which the city thrived. In 1788, Penny offered his views to a parliamentary committee set up to investigate the practice, stating that he had invested in no less than eleven voyages transporting human cargo from Africa to the West Indies. His ships carried 500–600 slaves per trip and helped make Penny a very rich man. Paul McCartney looked back on his memories of Penny Lane in a 2009 interview:

> Penny Lane was kind of nostalgic, but it was really a place that John and I knew; it was actually a bus terminus. I'd get a bus to his house and I'd have to change at Penny Lane, or the same with him to me, so we often hung out at that terminus, like a roundabout. It was a place that we both knew, and so we both knew the things that turned up in the story.

The lyrics to 'Penny Lane' are particularly descriptive. The shelter in the middle of the roundabout had been built on the site of a historic delph in the 1930s, and by the time Lennon and McCartney knew it, was a main route for public transport in and out of town. The structure was originally a tram ticket office and has a distinctive art deco aesthetic. The banker with the motorcar referred to in the song could have been employed by one of three banks that operated here at the time, and the fireman with the hourglass is likely to have been from the station in nearby Mather Avenue. It is thought that the pretty nurse selling poppies from a tray may well have been a girl by the name of Beth Davidson, who Lennon knew in his youth and actually sold poppies in her cadet uniform near to Bioletti's barber's shop, also mentioned in the lyrics. Lennon had spent his early years living in Newcastle Road very close to the places of Penny Lane and he walked past the shelter to and from school while growing up. During his time with the Quarrymen Lennon played at St Barnabas's Church on several occasions, and Paul had even been a choirboy there. As such, Penny Lane was a very familiar place to both Beatles throughout their youth.

Penny Lane, like many parts of the city has changed considerably since the release of the record in 1967, but several song locations still remain to be seen. The shelter remains standing in the middle of the roundabout and has become something of an attraction to Beatles fans, with road signs often vanishing as souvenirs. In the 1980s, the old shelter was bought by a private developer who seized upon the opportunity to extend the building in

Penny Lane depicted four decades after the Beatles' eponymous musical release.

This area of Penny Lane described in the band's descriptive melody includes 'the shelter in the middle of the roundabout'.

a bid to create a small restaurant – Sgt. Pepper's Bistro. Unfortunately, the venture was unsuccessful and the structure fell into disuse, becoming something of an eyesore. The Fab Four landmark has been the subject of a number of planning proposals and today features a glass dining area on what was the original roof, providing views out to Penny Lane and the surrounding streets. Despite various attempts at finding a use for the former shelter, it remains closed. The barbers made famous by the band for 'showing photographs of every head he's had the pleasure to know' continues to trade but is now known as Tony Slavin's. Just one bank remains in operation in this particular location, but the number of motor cars has most definitely increased around this very busy part of the city. The modern view was also taken at the junction of Dovedale Road and features the imposing structure of Dovedale Towers. This building is now a bar and restaurant, but had originally been a private residence known as Grove House owned by a wealthy merchant. Over the years it has served many purposes from an orphanage, to a Russian embassy, to a dance hall. When the building was under the control of St Barnabas's Church in the 1950s the Quarrymen played as a skiffle group to the crowds at Saturday night dances. In 2006, a local councillor proposed that, in light of its insalubrious connections to slavery, the world-famous Penny Lane should be renamed. This idea was rejected with a consensus that the city's heritage, however unsavoury, should not be airbrushed or the subject of political masquerade.

Liverpool's famous Penny Lane seen at the corner of Dovedale Road in the 1960s.

25. THE BLUECOAT SCHOOL

The Bluecoat School is the oldest building in Liverpool City Centre and dates from 1717. It was founded several years earlier by Revd Robert Stythe and wealthy sea captain Bryan Blundell. Blundell made a fortune in the transatlantic slave trade and also served as mayor of Liverpool for two separate terms. The Bluecoat was established with charity in mind and with the aim of teaching poor children in the area to read, write and cast accounts. At this time poverty and destitution was rife in the port town, and the institution later began operating as a boarding school to further look after its young scholars. Many of the children who studied here went on to be apprenticed to local tradesman, with a large percentage entering the multitude of maritime-related businesses the town was renowned for. The school became so successful that staff and students were required to relocate to nearby Wavertree into bigger and better-equipped premises. The Bluecoat later became home to an independent art school and in 1911, a special exhibition featuring works by Picasso, Cézanne, Van Gogh, Matisse and Gauguin went on display. Tragedy struck in 1941 when the building caught fire after being struck by an incendiary bomb. The concert hall and adjoining rooms were severely damaged but luckily the building itself remained standing. From the 1960s onwards the Bluecoat reinvented itself as the stimulating hub of Liverpool's art scene. Yoko Ono famously put on an interactive exhibition in what was her first-ever paid performance on 26 September 1967. She bizarrely invited audience members on stage to carry out such acts as jumping off ladders, chalking messages on a blackboard and finally wrapping her in bandages in an exhibition she called 'Music of the Mind'. She had met John Lennon at a London exhibition several months earlier, leaving the Beatle intrigued, curious and wanting to know more. Their friendship blossomed and the pair married in 1969, leading to controversial influences over the Beatles and their work.

The Bluecoat still stands after 300 years and remains as one of Merseyside's leading arts centres. In 2008, Yoko Ono returned to Liverpool to give a special one-hour live performance to reopen the Bluecoat after its £12.5 million refurbishment, timed to coincide with the city's Capital of Culture celebrations. Just 200 tickets were allocated for the event, which sold out within minutes, so it was agreed that a live feed of her performance would be beamed onto a big screen in the city centre. The avant-garde artist picked up where she had left off years before, this time inviting the audience to remove bandages from her body, while footage of her original exhibition, her 1969 'bed-in' with John and some of her shorter documentaries were played overhead. The hour-long performance concluded with fans being asked to dance with the seventy-five-year-old to a remix of 'Give Peace a Chance'. Prior to this she opened a participatory installation, inviting visitors to share their wishes and tie them to the branches of a specially planted tree in the Bluecoat garden.

Above: The Bluecoat School dates from 1717 and is the oldest building in Liverpool city centre.

Below: Yoko Ono returned to the city in 2008 to give a special performance at the recently refurbished venue.

Those scraps of paper were later taken to Iceland and buried alongside a million others under Yoko's Imagine Peace Tower. Looking back Yoko said, 'I fell in love with Liverpool the first time I went there in 1967 as an artist. When I arrived in Liverpool, the first thing that caught my eyes was the beautiful, old elegance of the city by the water. Performing at the Bluecoat is an experience I have never forgotten.' Her marriage to John resulted in the birth of their son Sean in 1975, and since his death she has continued to work to preserve John's memory around the world.

John Lennon and Yoko Ono seen together in 1969, the same year in which they married.

26. THE ALBERT DOCK

The Albert Dock dates back long before the Beatles ever played a single note, but this collection of Victorian warehouses have become just as much a part of Liverpool's culture as the boys themselves. Most notably it has even become home to the city's official Beatles Museum, celebrating the life of the band and their extraordinary achievements. Plans for a dock were originally developed by civil engineer Jesse Hartley, who was the world's first professional dock engineer. He prepared designs for pioneering fireproof warehouses in order to combat the risks involved in storing valuable cargo. Hartley followed the building philosophy of Lancashire's extensive textile mills, which faced similar issues with combustibility. In the nineteenth century, Liverpool had blossomed to become the second city of the British Empire and a leading trade port dealing with everything from brandy to wool. The town's place on the Mersey gave industrialists a distinct advantage over other merchant towns, with easy access to foreign markets. The dock complex would be unique in its ability to allow vessels to unload directly to and from the warehouses, and few Victorian industrial buildings would equal their splendour. The cast-iron columns that would keep these structures aloft were modelled on the Greek style, and materials such as stone, brick and iron helped limit the risk of fire as well as brick and tiled floors with thick dividing walls positioned within the storage rooms. The complex was officially opened by Queen Victoria's consort, Prince Albert in 1846 amid an array of pomp and splendour. It covered around 7.5 acres and cost the equivalent of £41 million in today's money.

The Albert Dock proved initially popular with traders across the world but its dimensions soon proved difficult for vessels transporting increasingly larger stock. The complex was designed to accommodate modest sailing ships but new steamships just could not navigate the limited waters. By the 1860s, the dock began to lose business and parts were converted for cold storage, signalling the beginning of the end of the dock's commercial heyday. The Second World War saw it transform into a base for naval vessels, including small warships, submarines, landing crafts and merchant boats. In 1940, a Nazi bomber flew over and released a parachute mine, causing serious damage to several sections. The following year an incendiary bomb exploded on the roof of the Atlantic Pavilion on the landward side of the complex and later bombing resulted in yet more damage during Liverpool's infamous May Blitz. Liverpool's musical fame put the city under a global spotlight throughout the 1960s, but this attention made little difference to the dock. Throughout the decade it became increasingly derelict, before being abandoned to the elements by 1972.

Today, the Albert Dock is a prosperous tourist attraction, having been given a new lease of life through a pioneering scheme of mixed-use development. Prior to its renaissance in the 1980s the Albert Dock was at real risk of demolition with a number of projects proposing a complete flattening of the site. One ambitious design hoped to bring about

The Albert Dock was a pioneering collection of warehouses built for Liverpool's entrepreneurial maritime merchants.

After decades of dereliction the Albert Dock has been transformed into a busy mixed-use development.

the construction of a dozen skyscrapers, built to house 50,000 workers in what was to be a standalone River City. Those plans were scaled back and rechristened Aquarius City but that, and other grand plans, failed to come to fruition. The works that did take place saw the dock saved and dredged of the accumulated silt that had amassed over years of neglect, along with the restoration of historic bridges and gates. Repairs were carried out to the original dock walls, as well as careful landscaping of the whole site. The tired neglected warehouses were fitted out to become apartments, shops, offices, galleries and museums in a multimillion-pound scheme between the Merseyside Development Corporation and Arrowcroft Group. One such museum that grew out of this urban resurgence was the Beatles Story, the world's largest permanent exhibition devoted to the achievements of the Fab Four. This can be found in the basement of the Britannia Pavilion, where it has been located since opening its doors for the first time in 1990. The museum charts the life of the band from childhood through to present day, with many unique and unusual artefacts on public display. Exhibitions include a pair of John Lennon's iconic round spectacles, items from the Beatles' personal wardrobes and even George Harrison's first guitar. The museum also offers visitors the chance to explore a replica of the Cavern Club and take a break in a mock-up of the Casbah. The Living History tour is narrated by John Lennon's half-sister Julia, and recordings of key figures like Brian Epstein, George Martin and Allan Williams help bring the Beatles' story to life. The museum has been recognised as one of the country's top attractions and entices thousands of fans, all eager to discover how four ordinary boys from the streets of Liverpool managed to conquer the world of music.

The Beatles Story is the world's largest permanent exhibition purely devoted to the lives and times of the band.

PICTURE CREDITS

My thanks to Mirrorpix, the Salvation Army International Heritage Centre and the region's local record offices, which have assisted in providing many of the historic images used in this publication, and to Bob Edwards for those of the modern era. Photographs of the Beatles and associated images have been published many times over the decades, and it is not always possible to ascertain who took them or presently owns the copyright over certain images. Copyright holders of images in this book if known have been contacted, but in the event of any oversight I shall be pleased to credit relevant copyright holders in future editions.

ALSO BY THE AUTHOR

 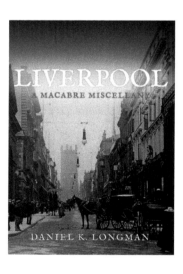

Liverpool in the Headlines
9 781 4456 4886 6

Liverpool: A Macabre Miscellany
9 781 4456 4694 7

Available to order direct 01453 847 800
www.amberley-books.com